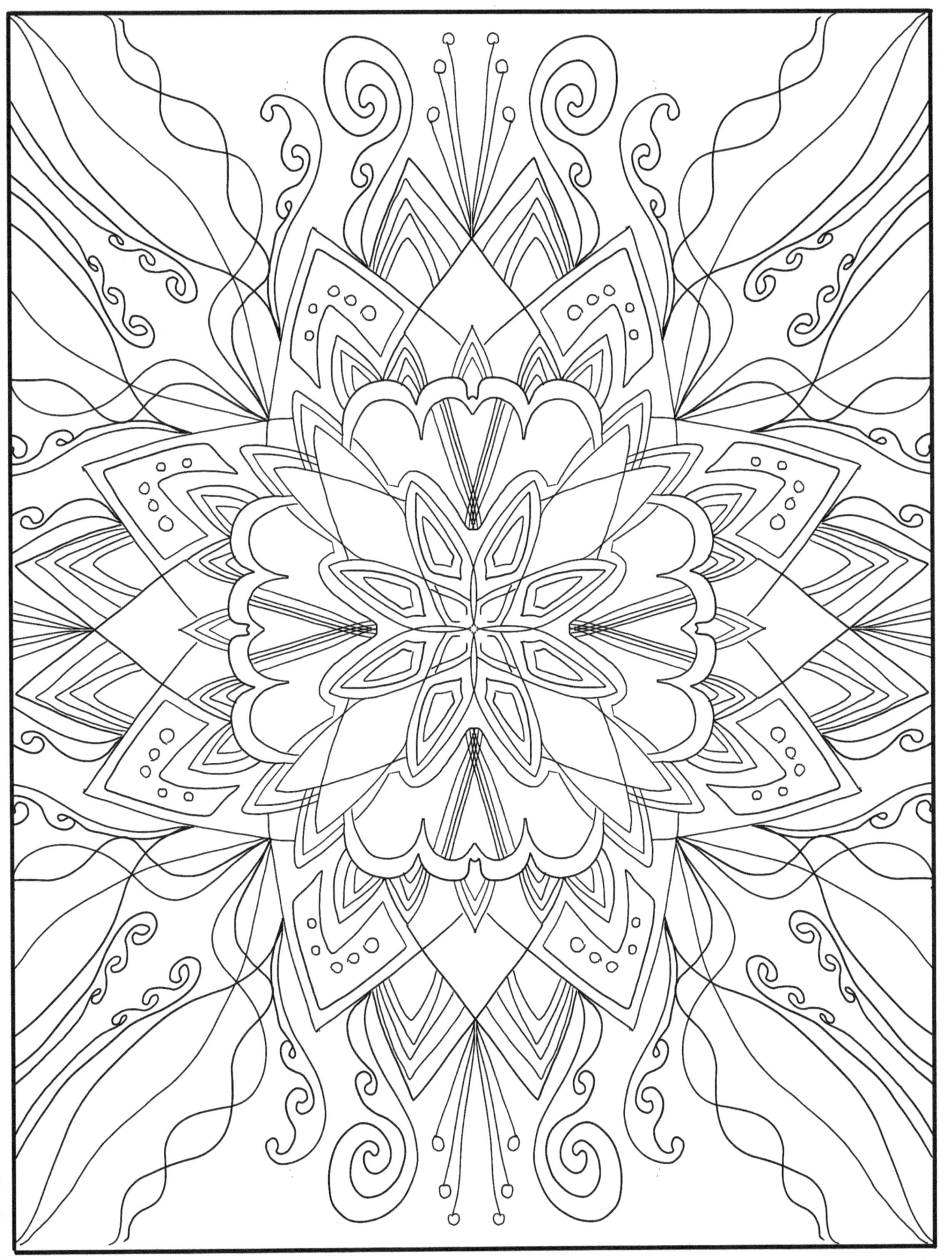

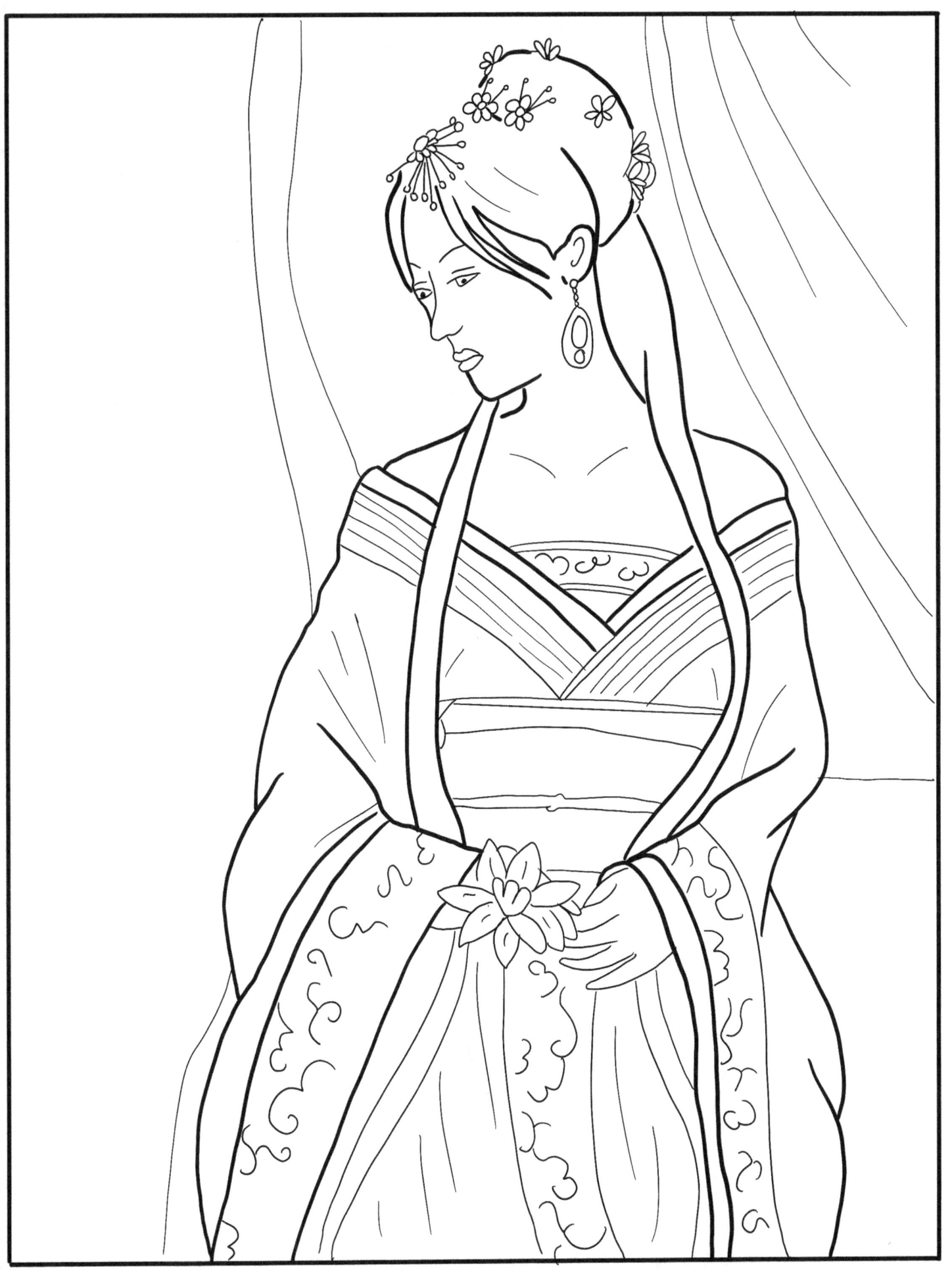

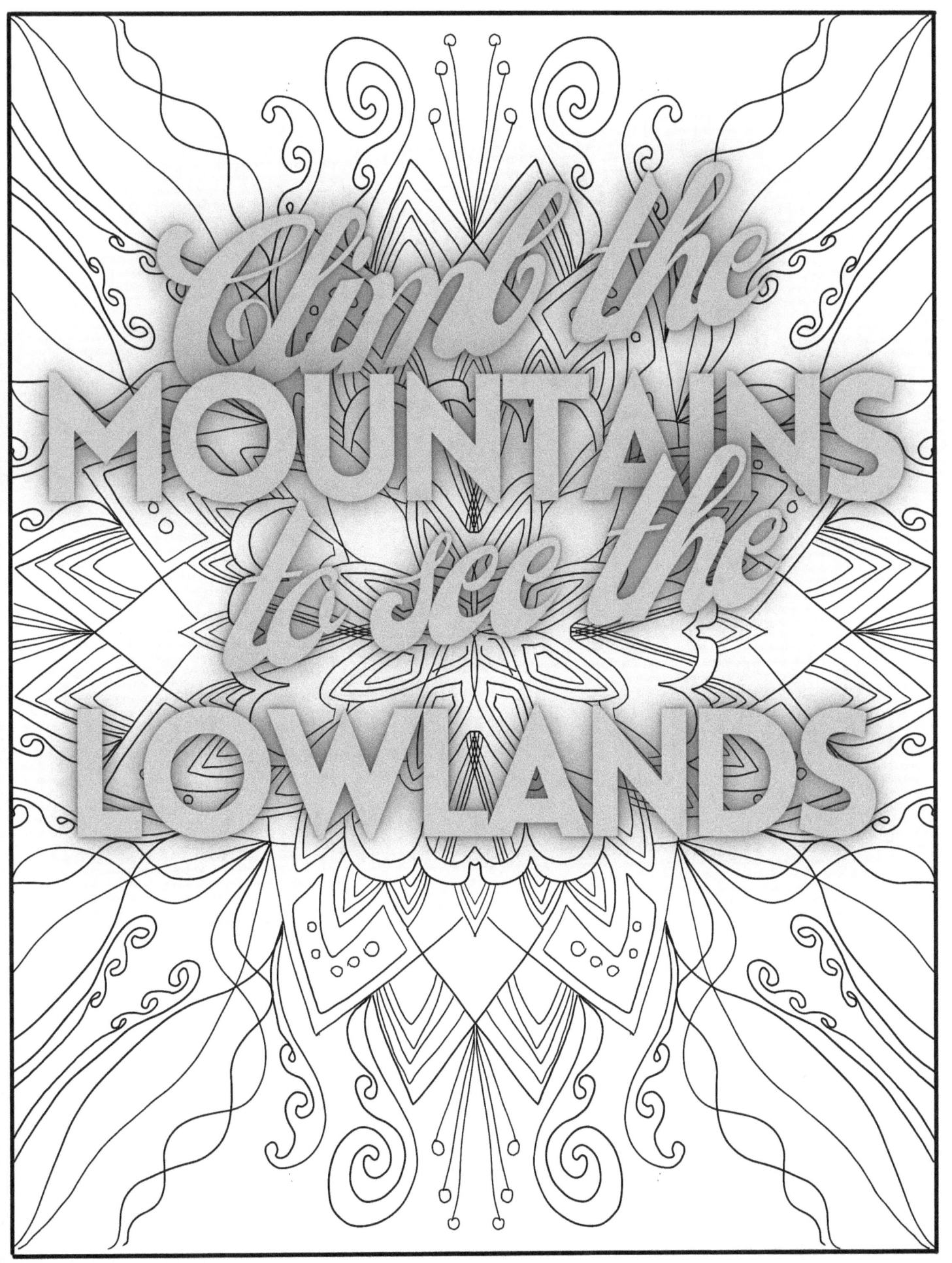

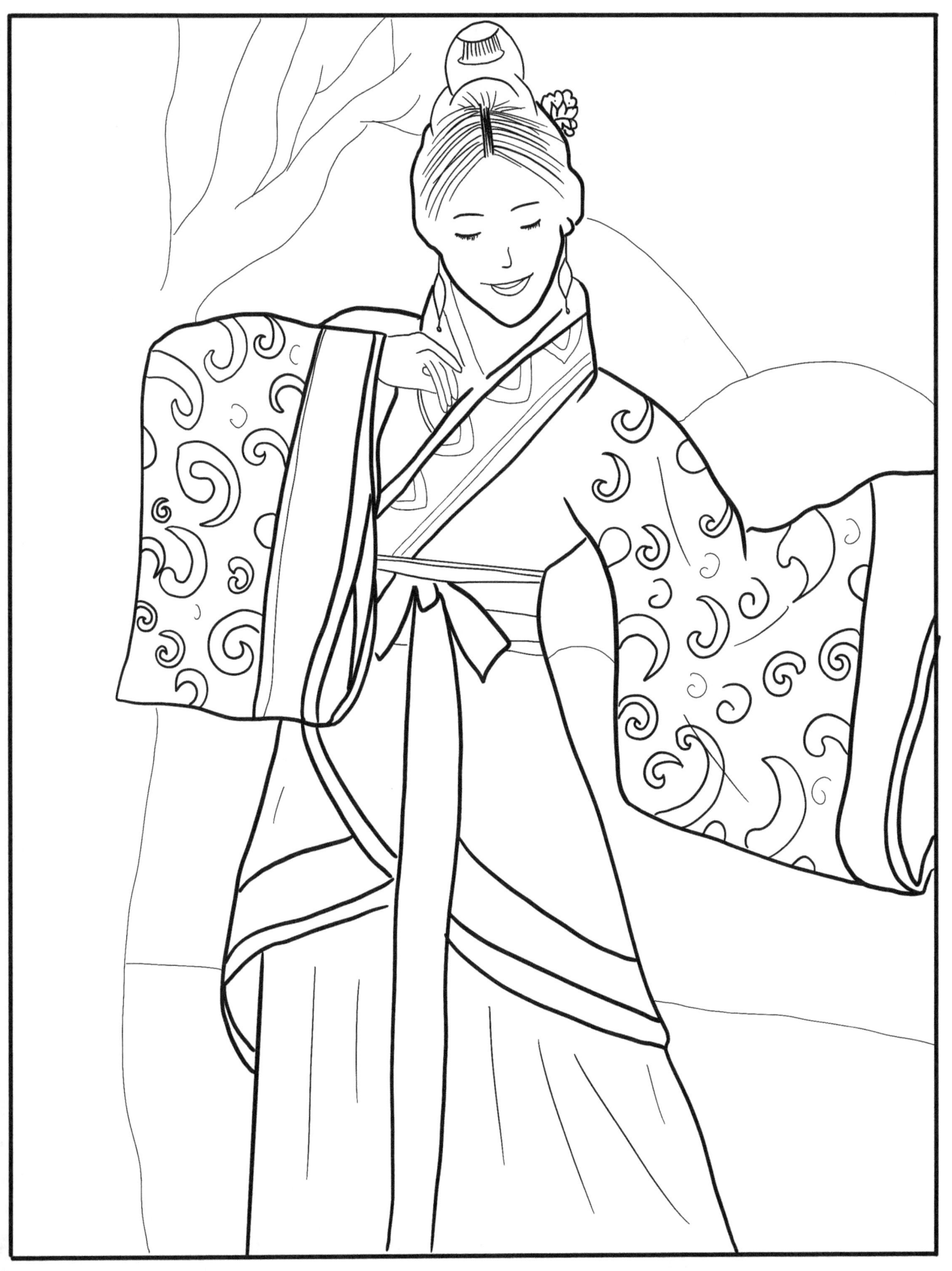

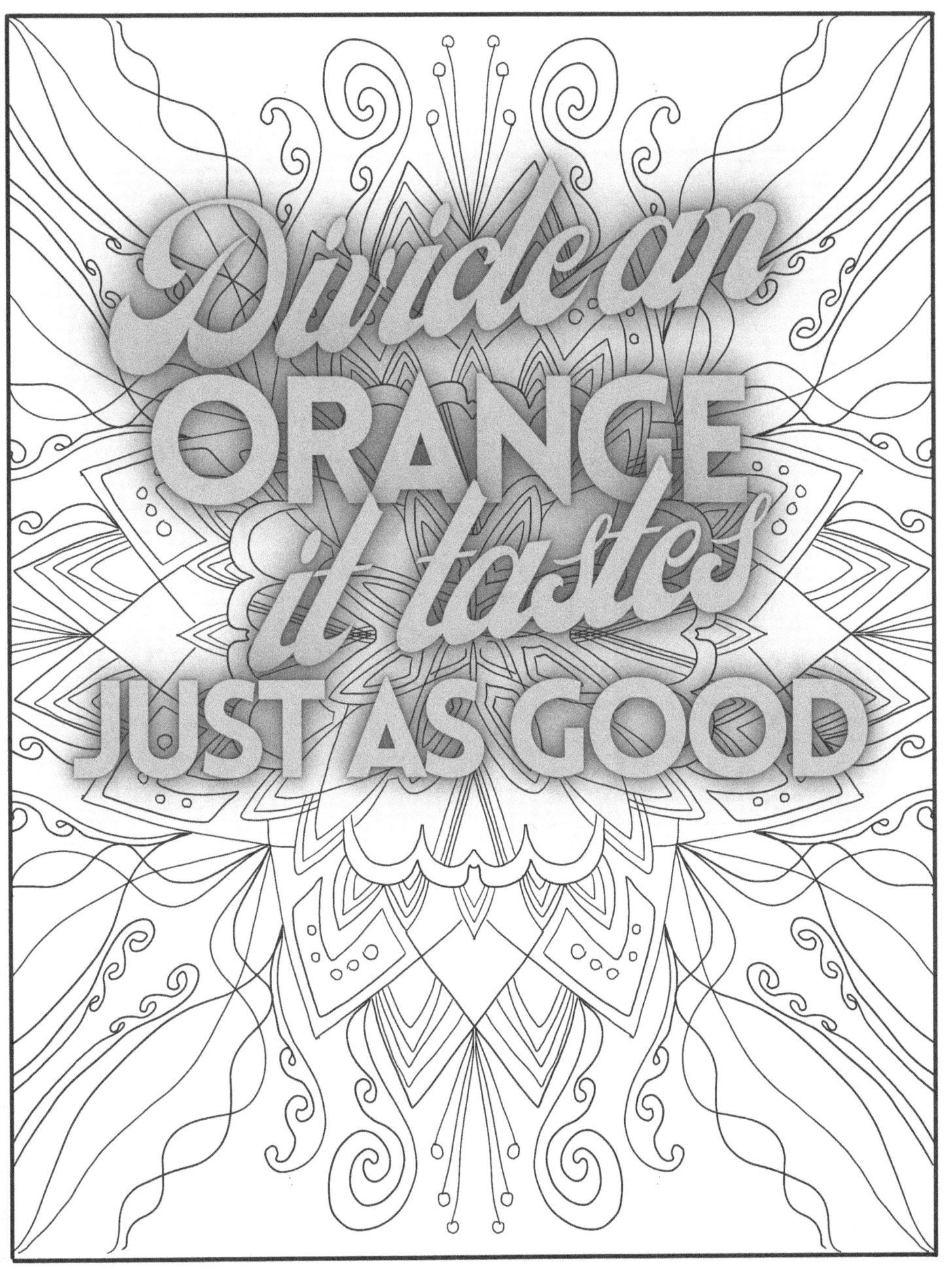

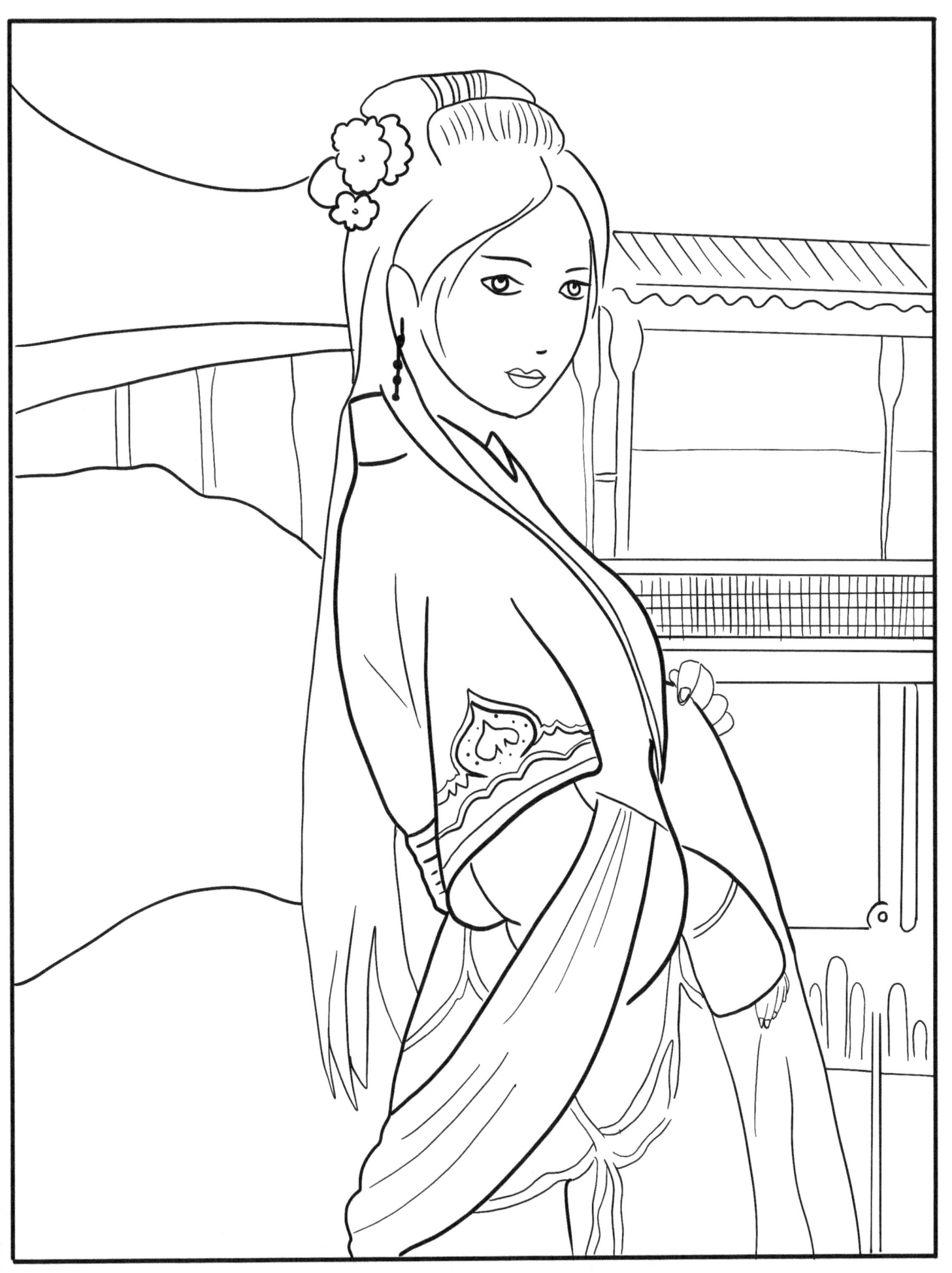

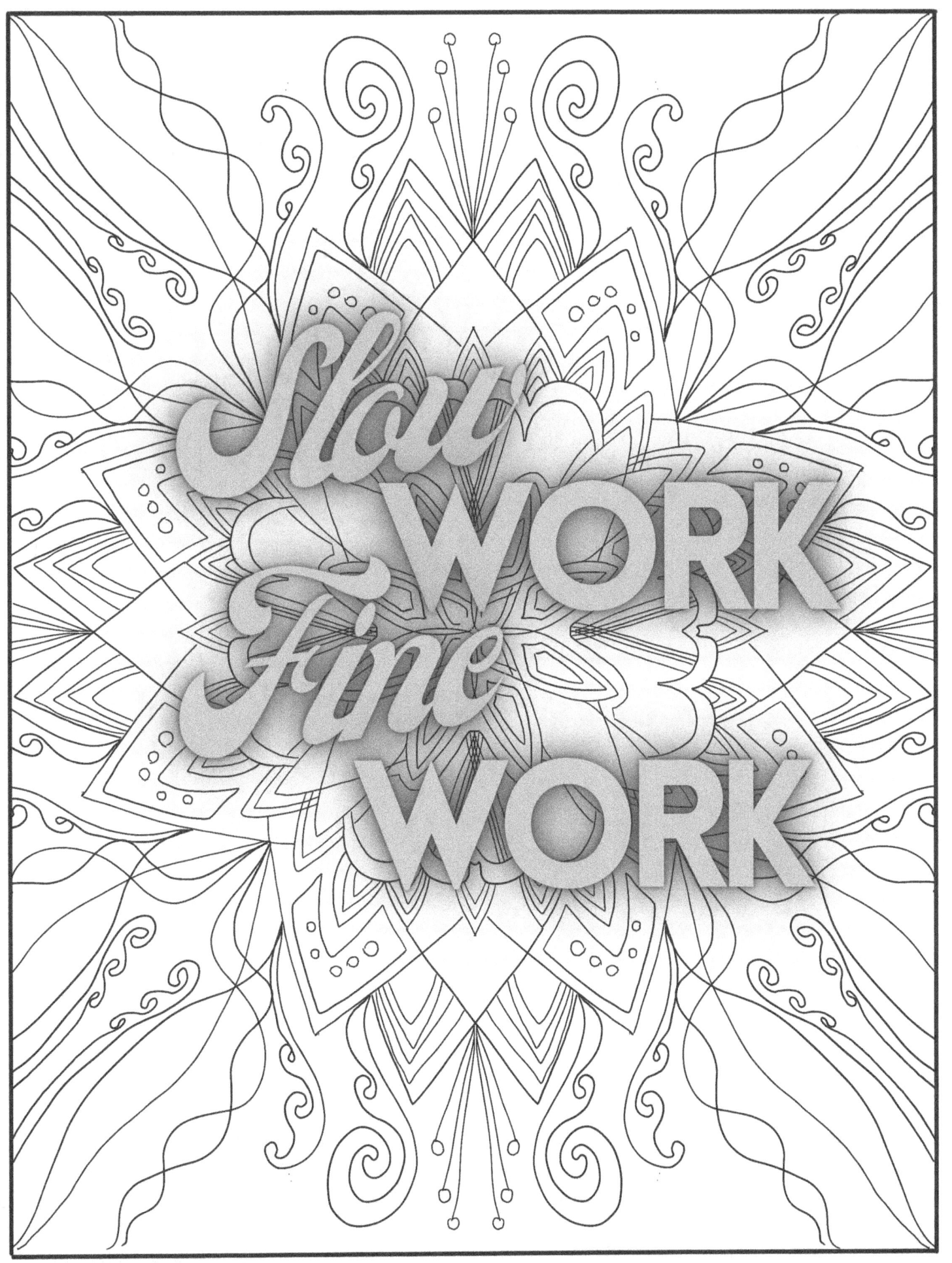

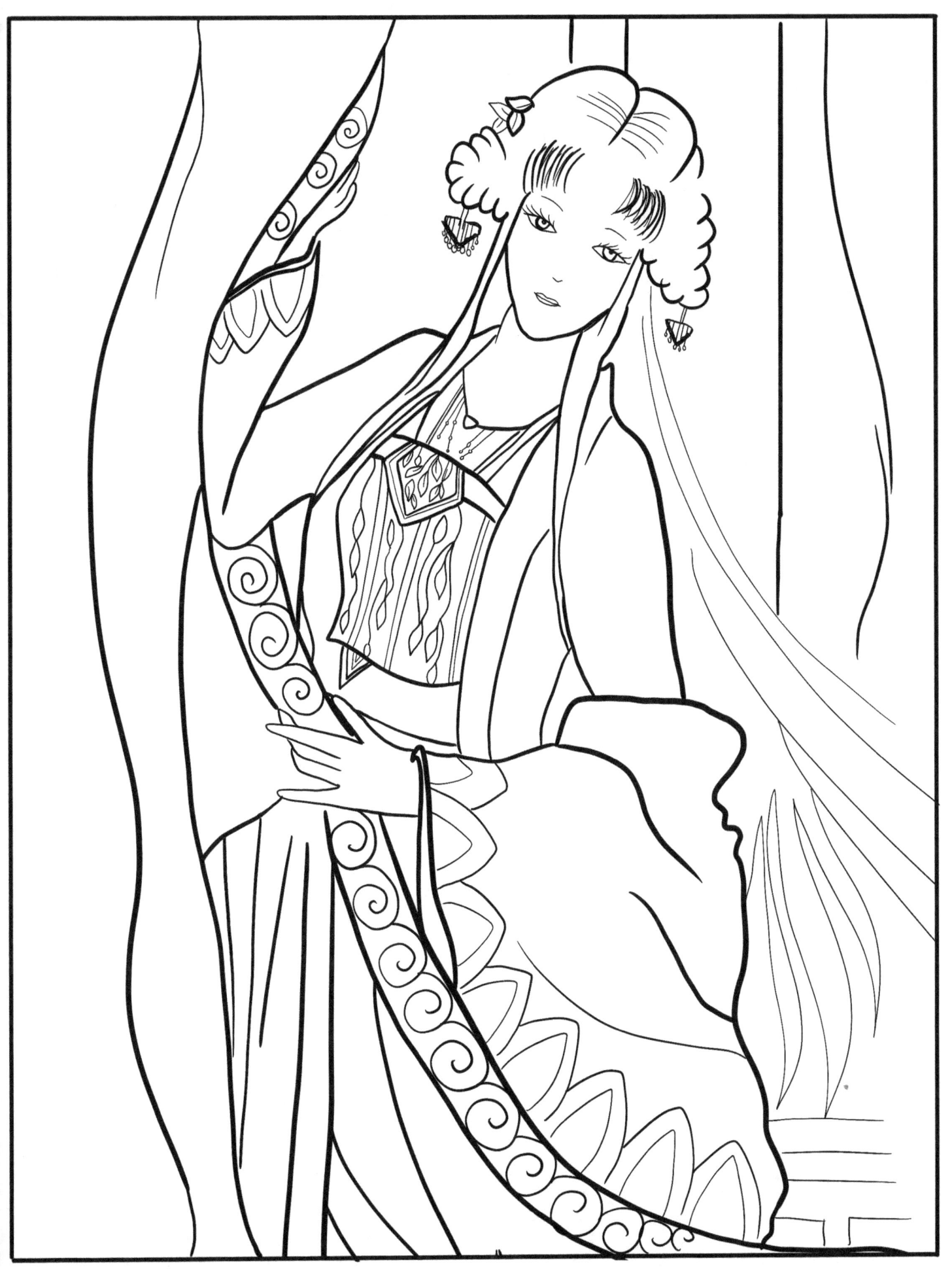

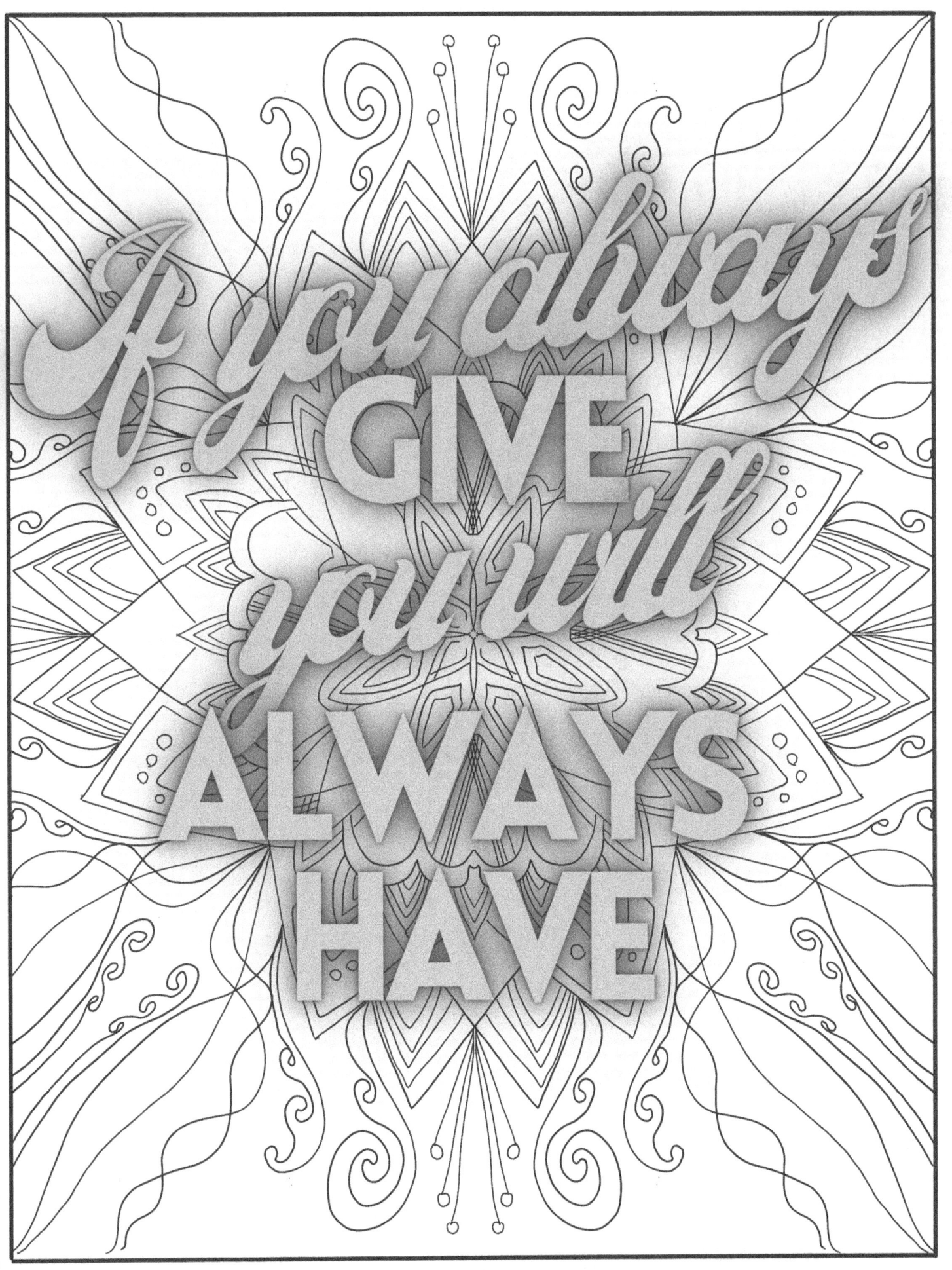

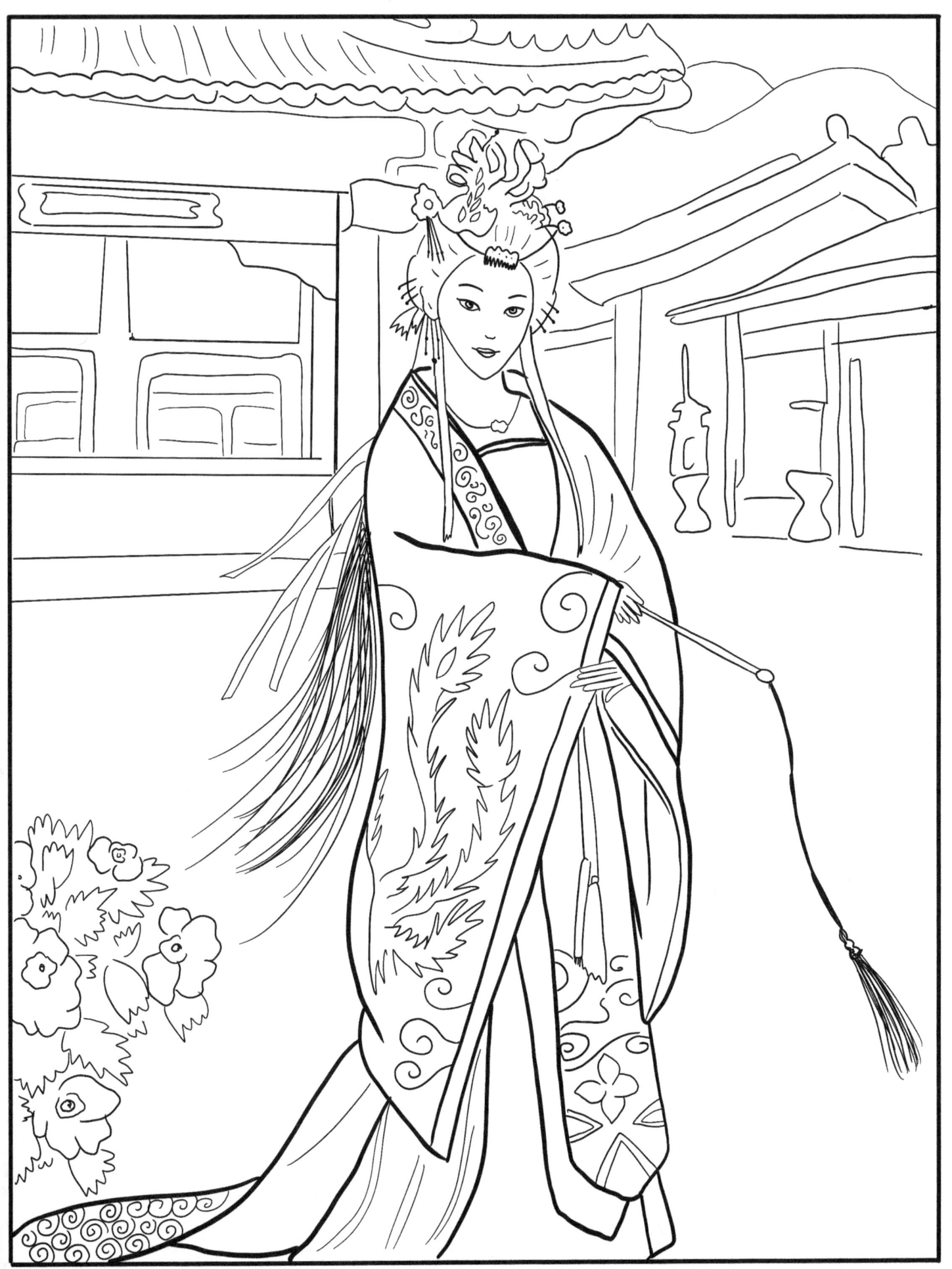

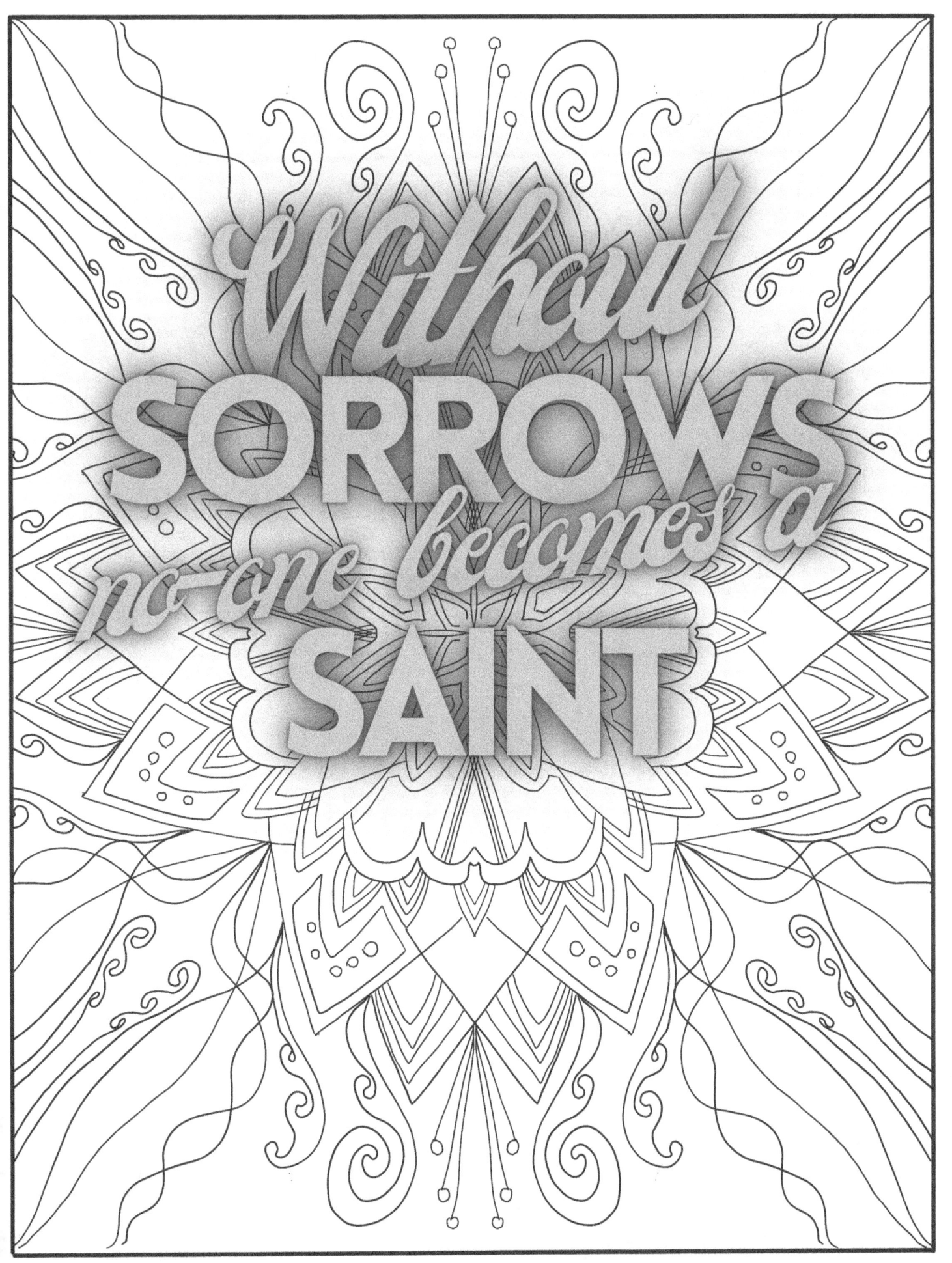

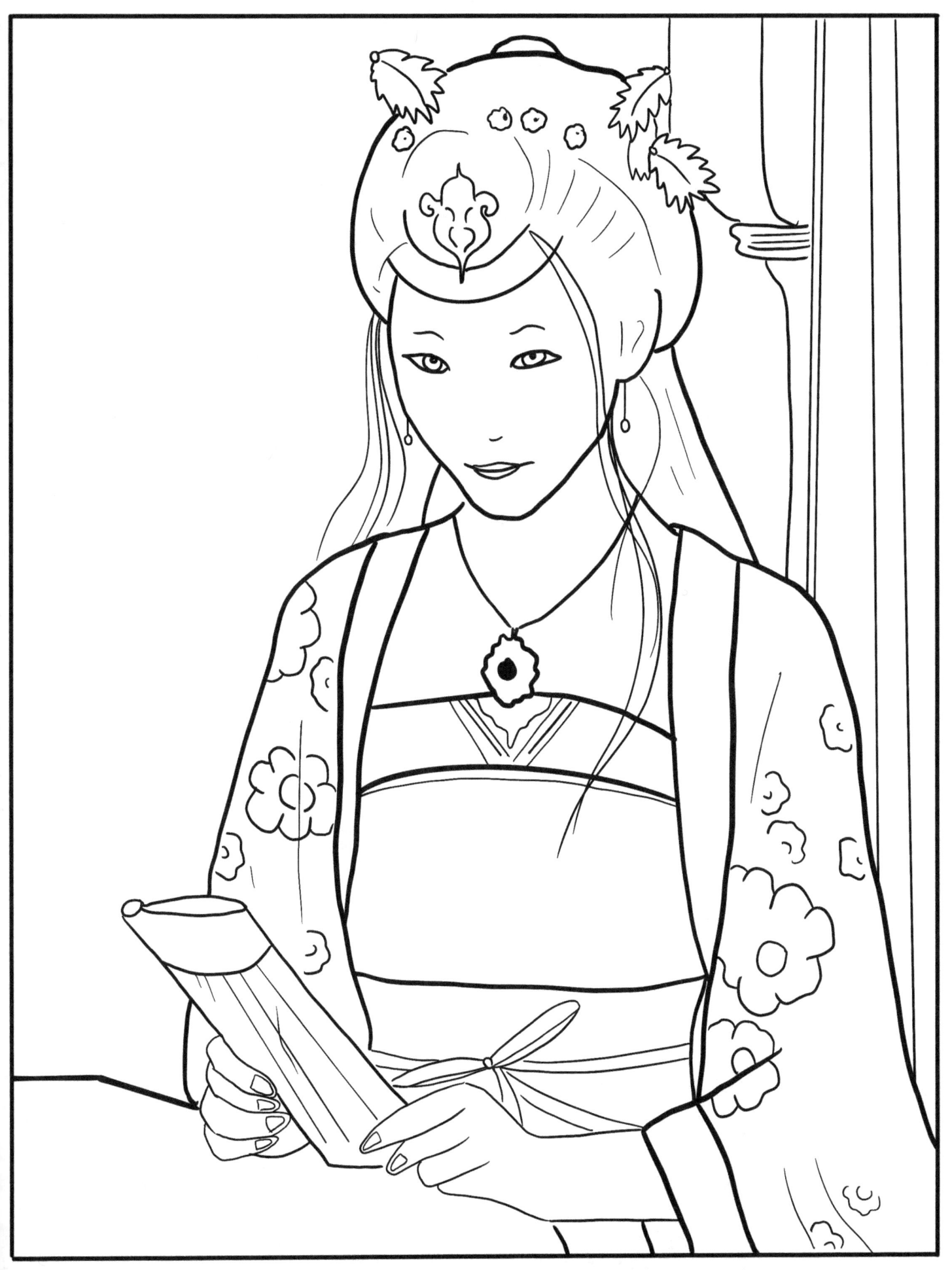

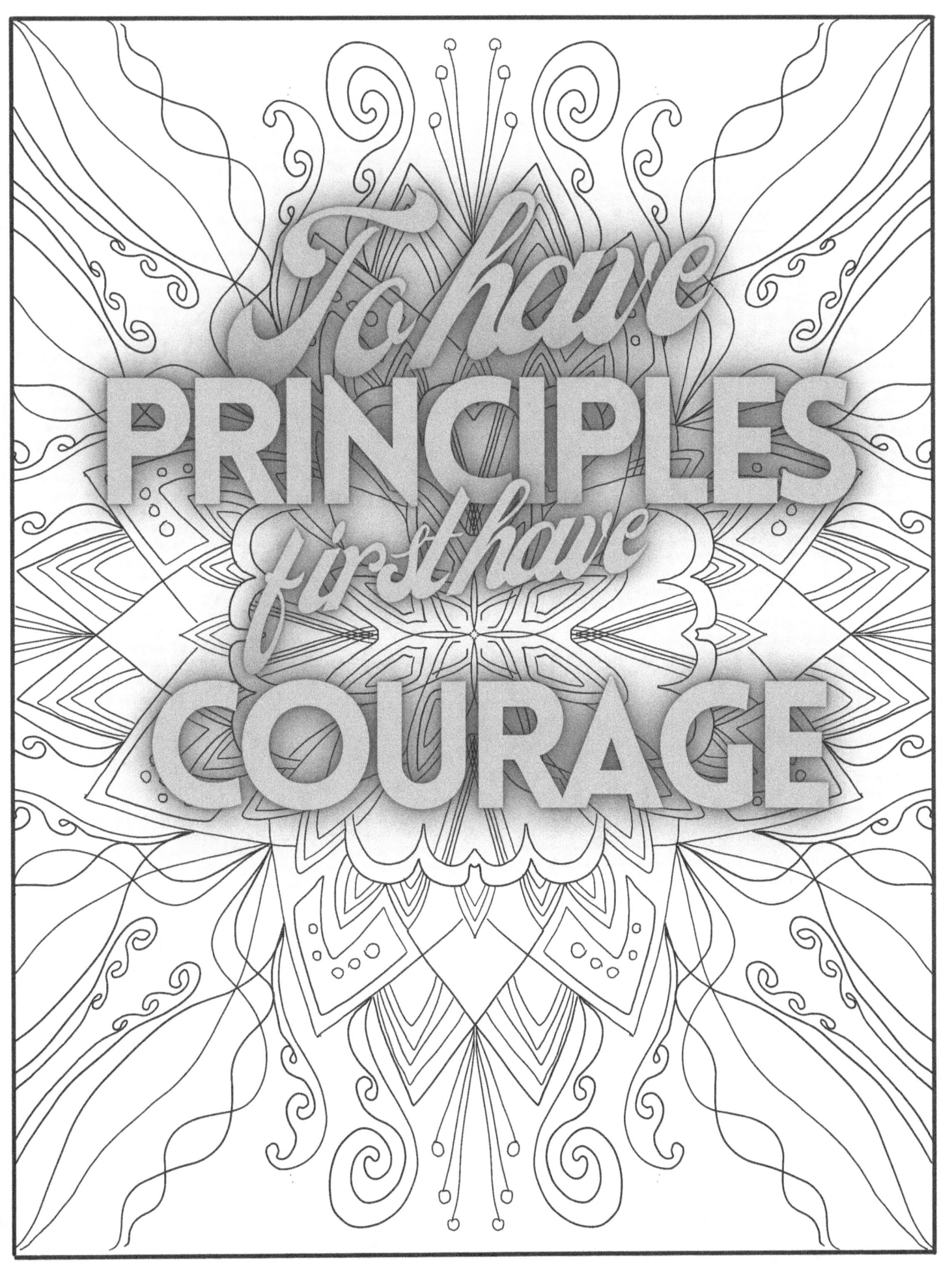

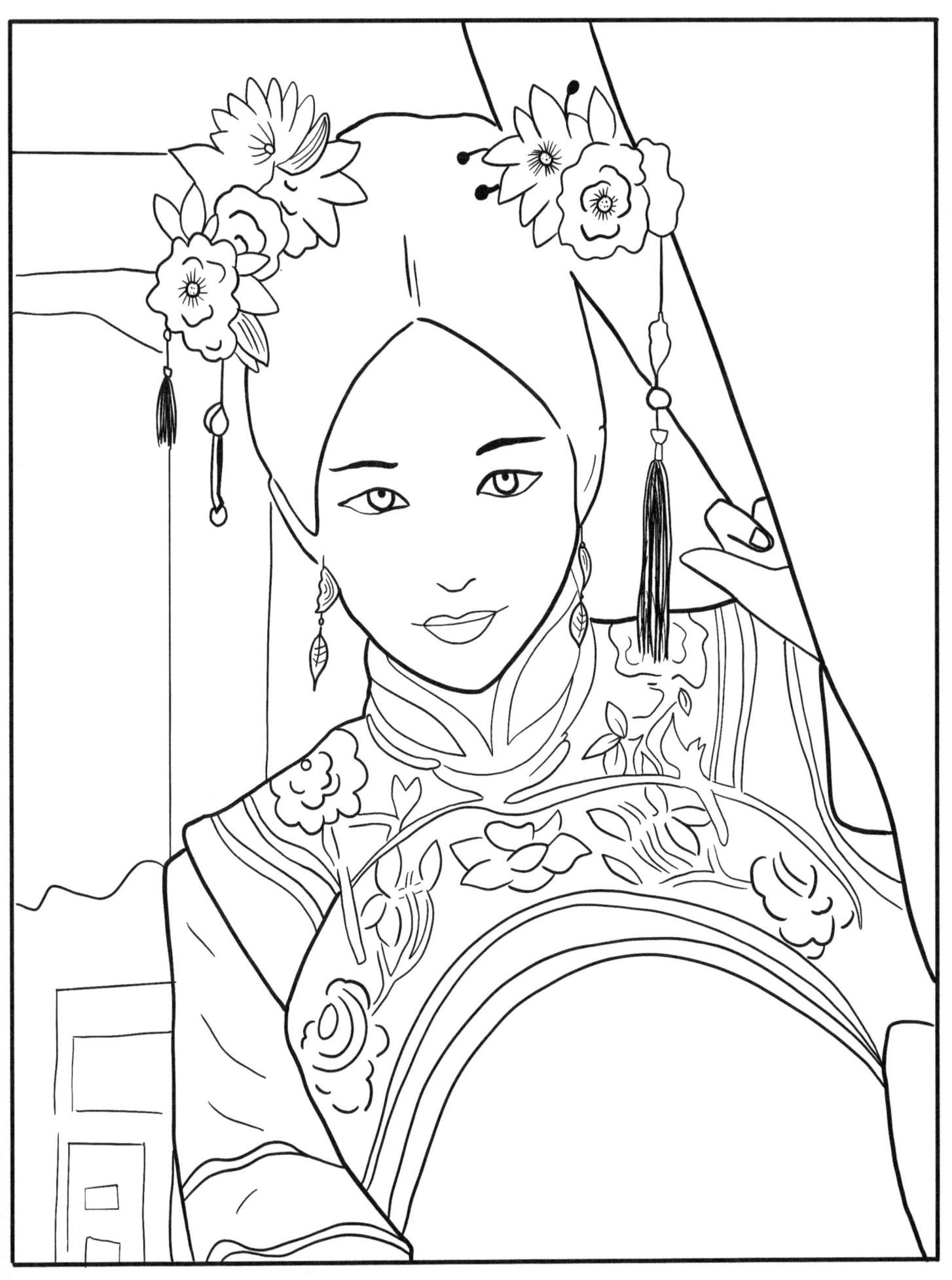

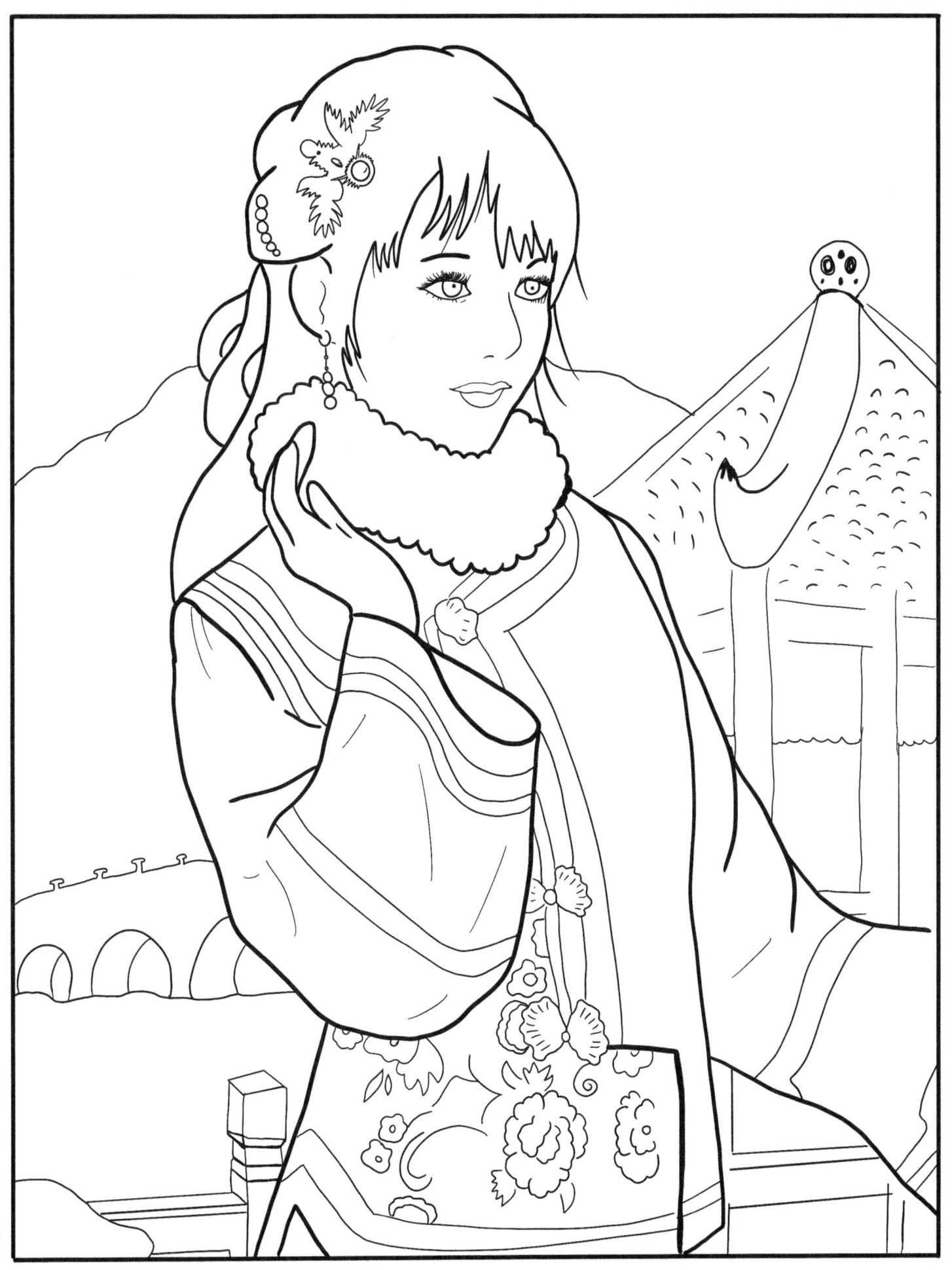

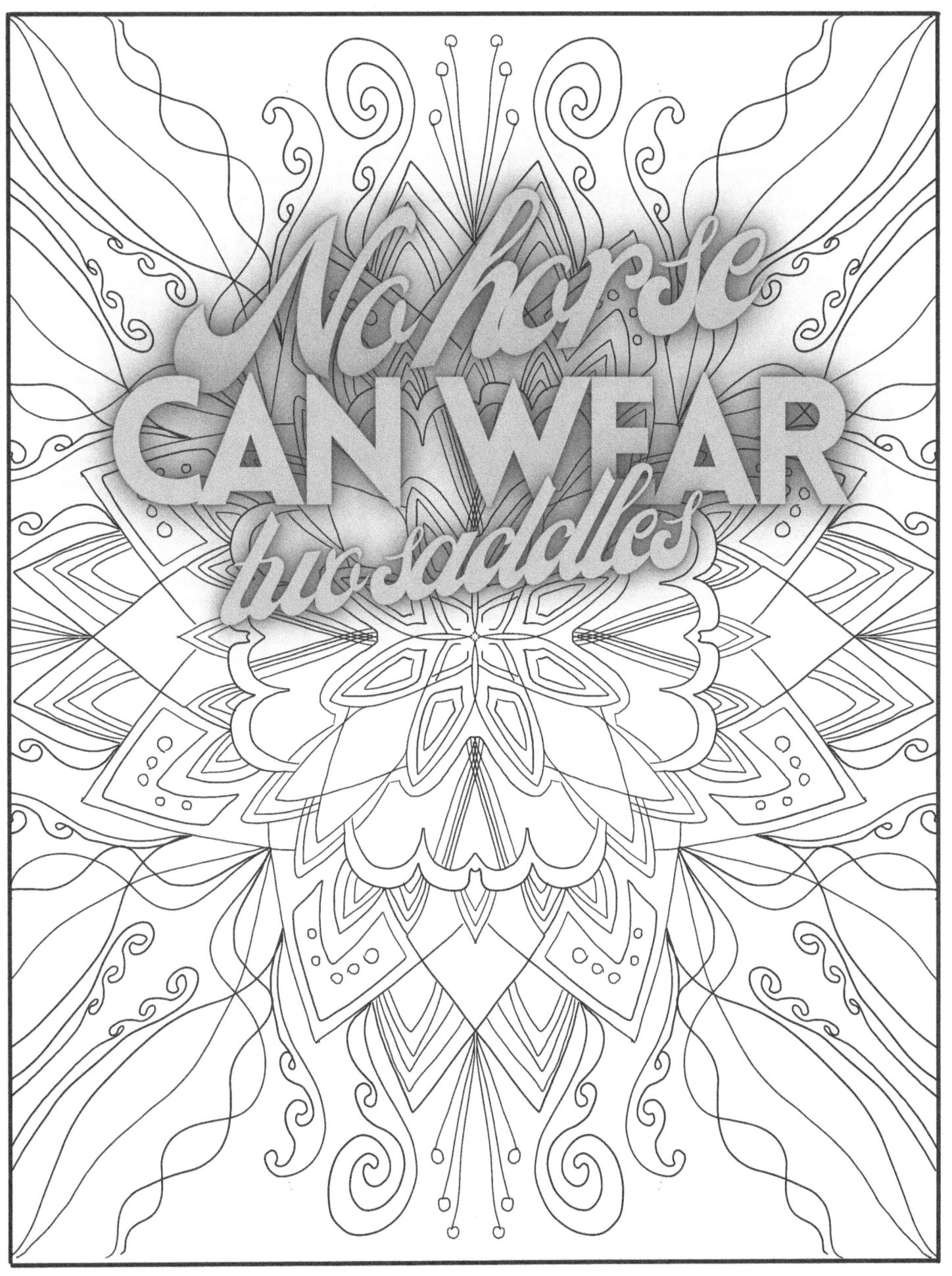

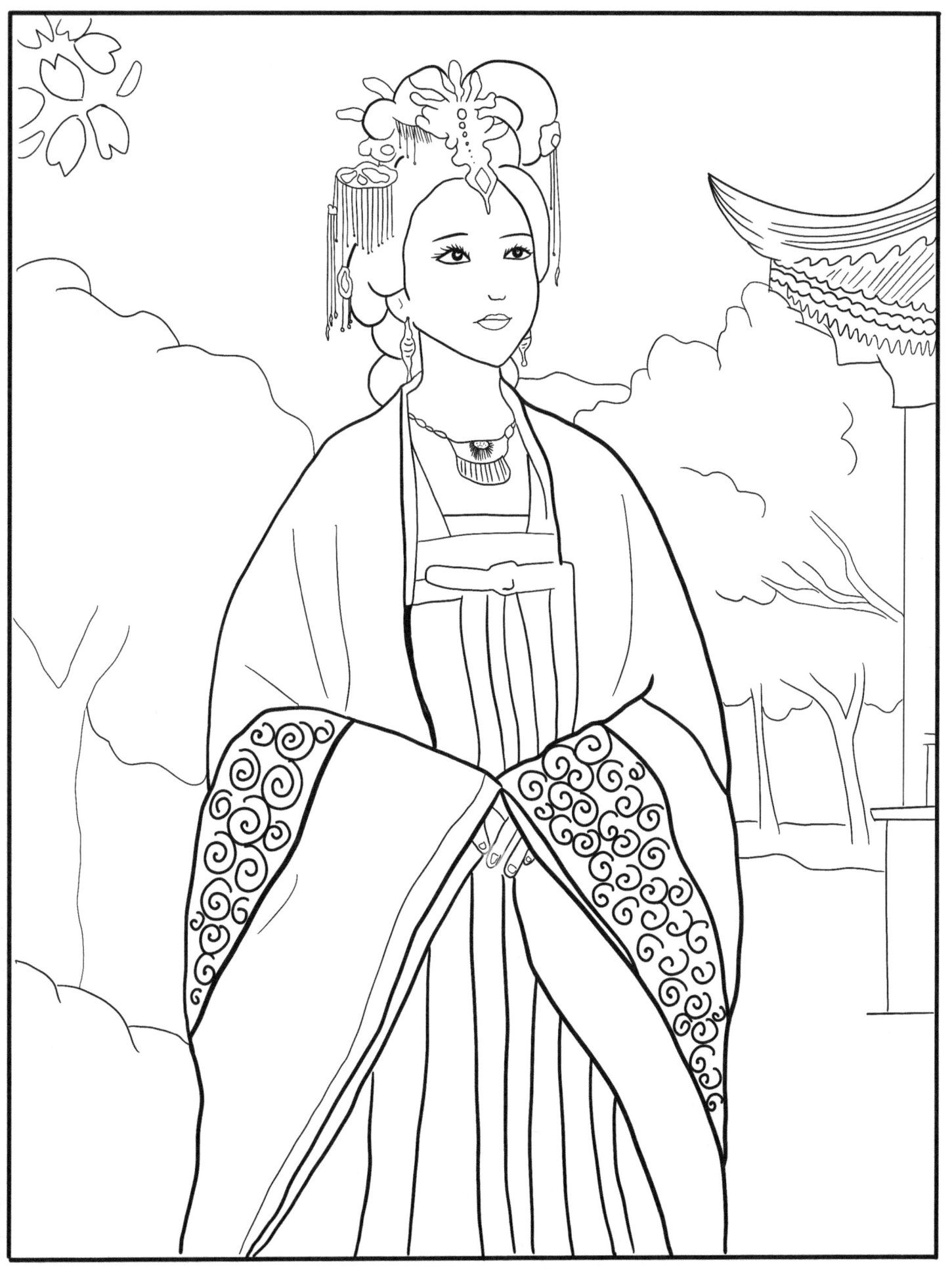

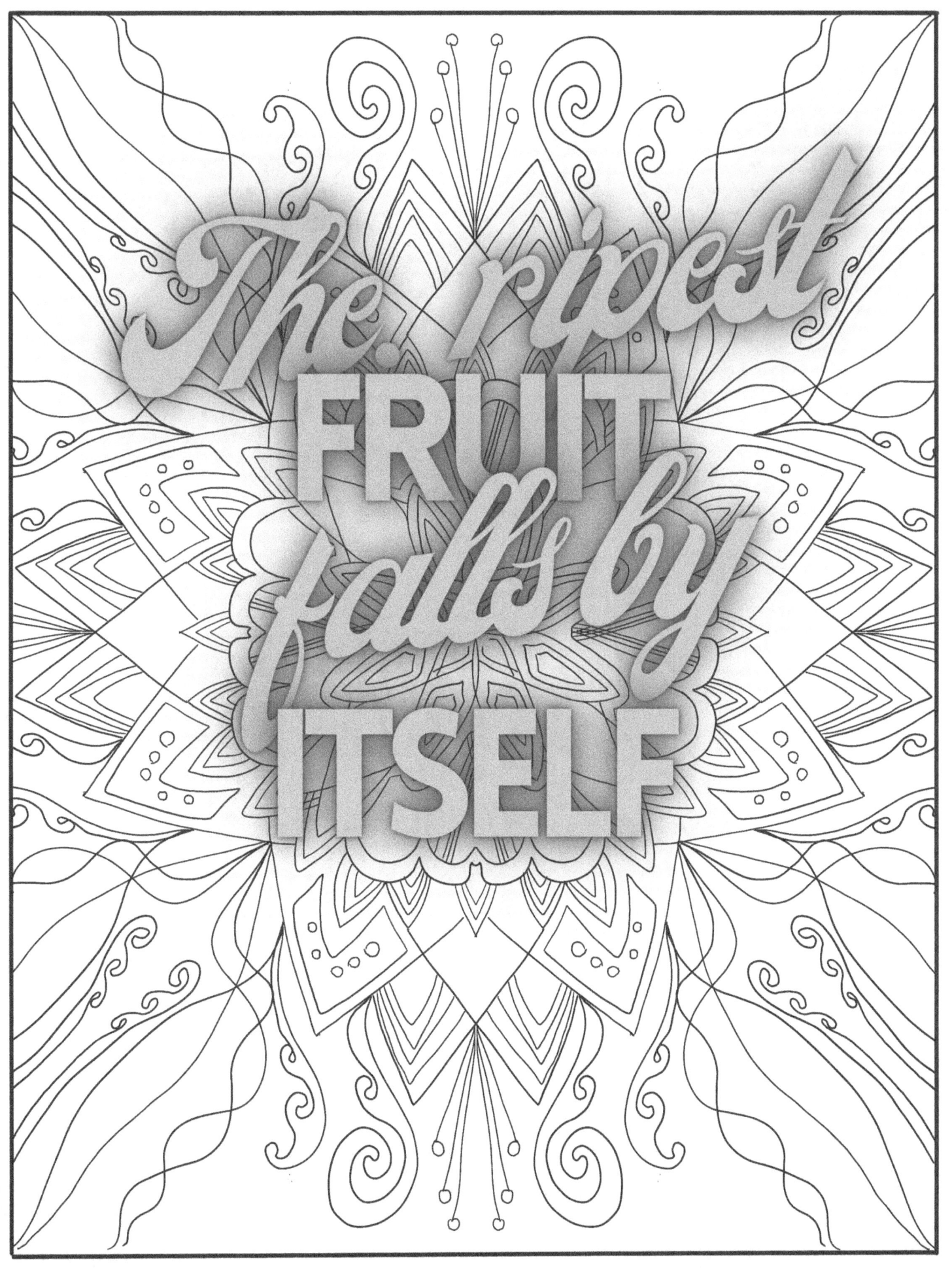

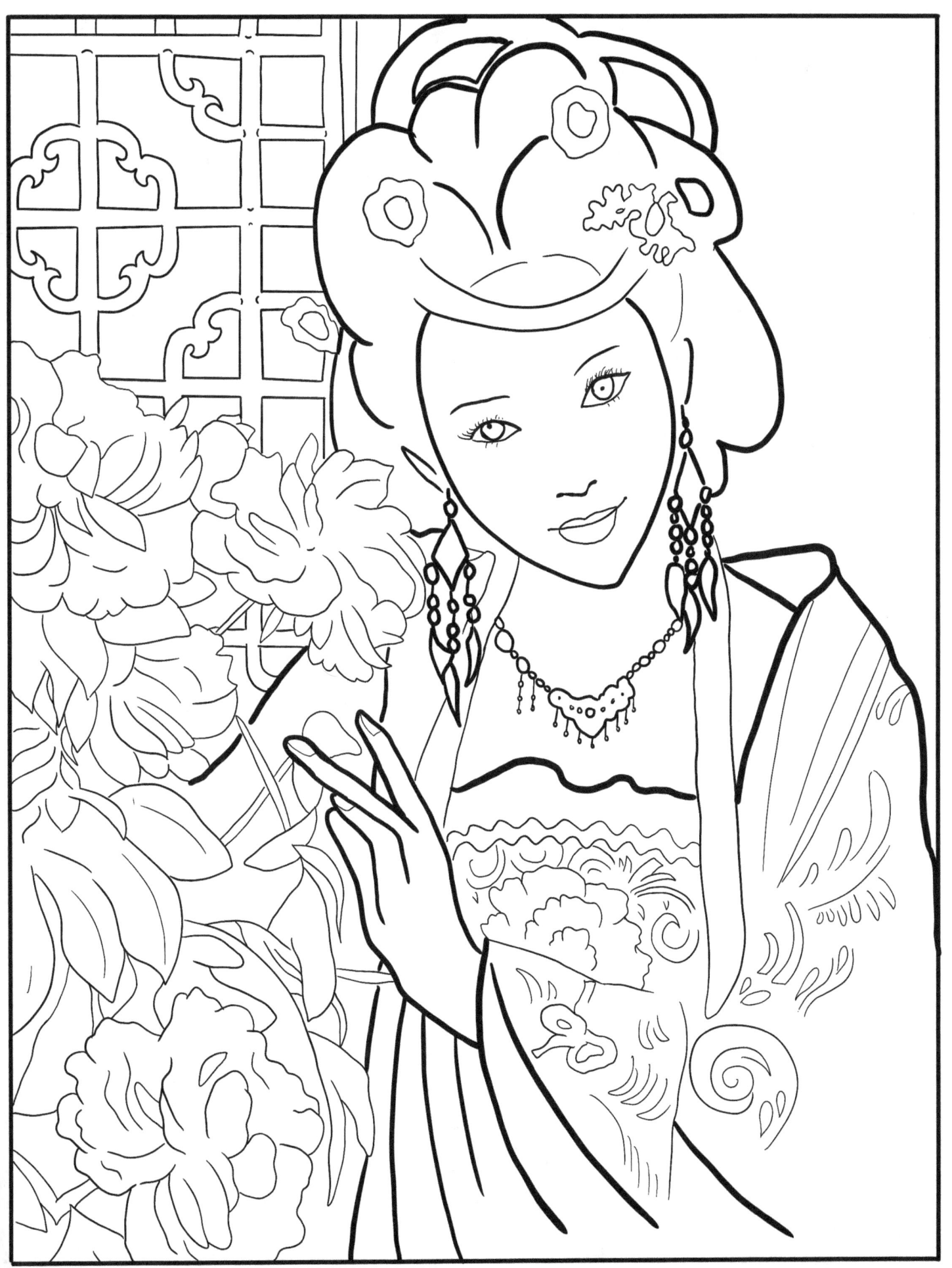

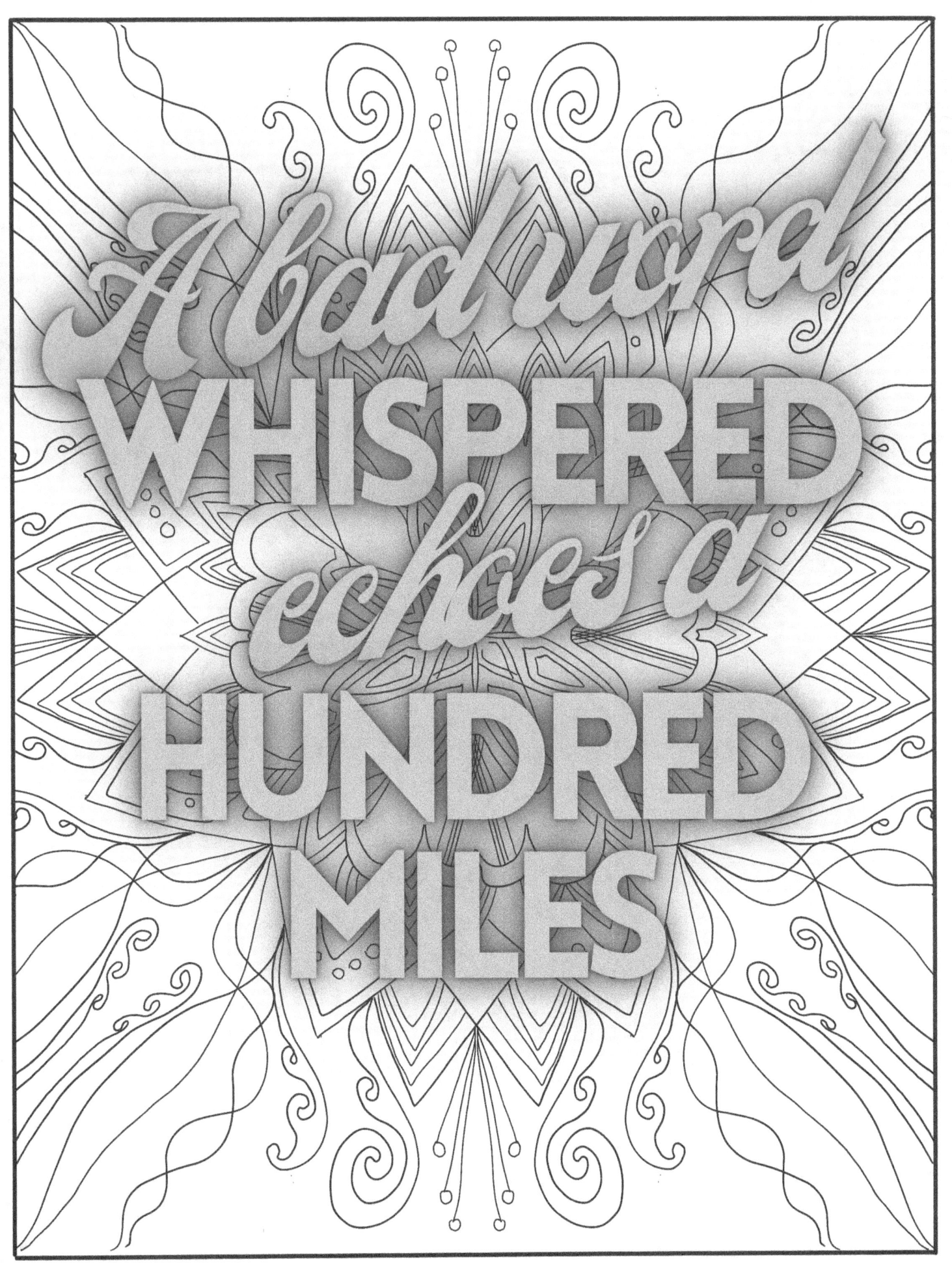

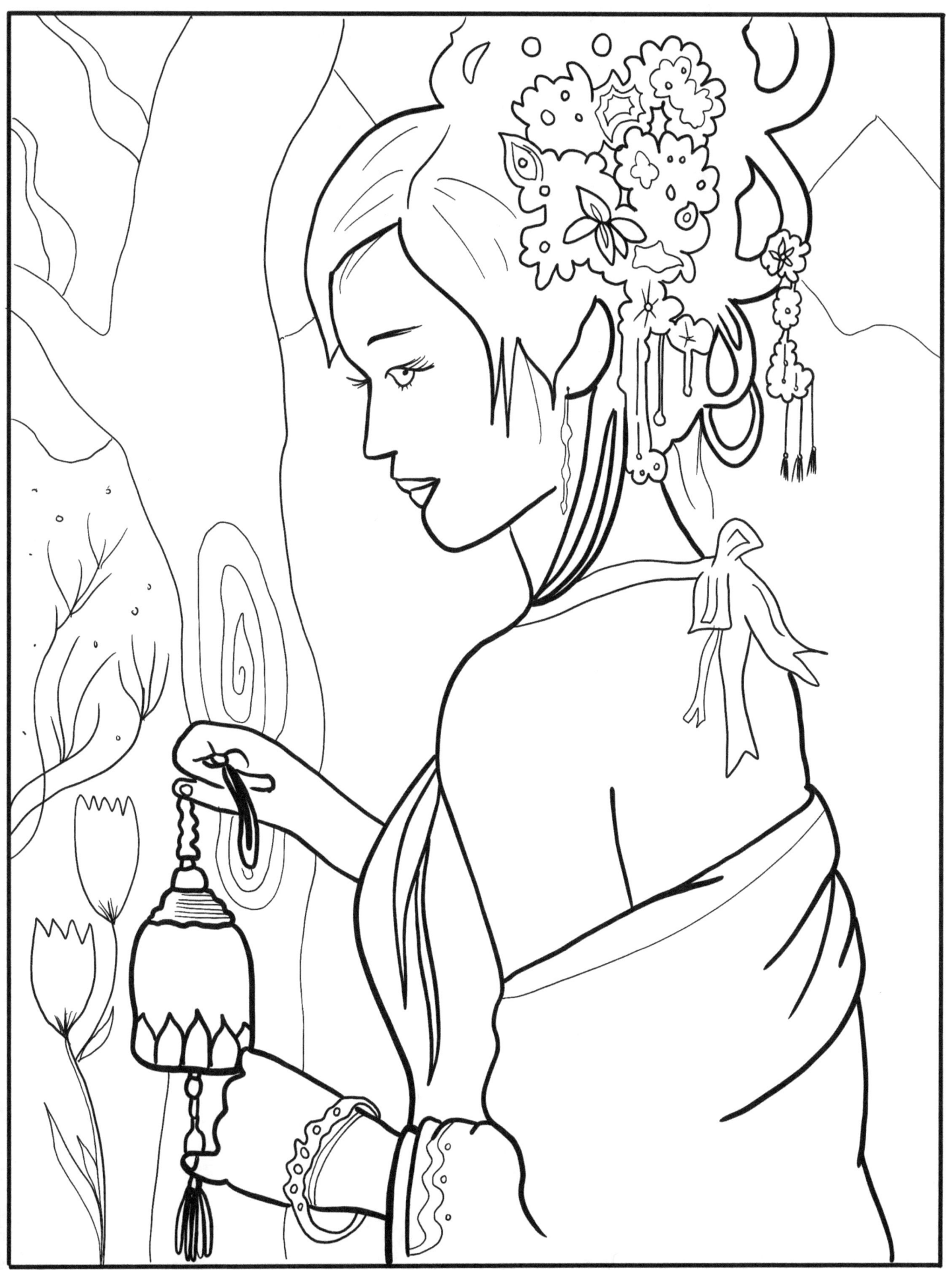

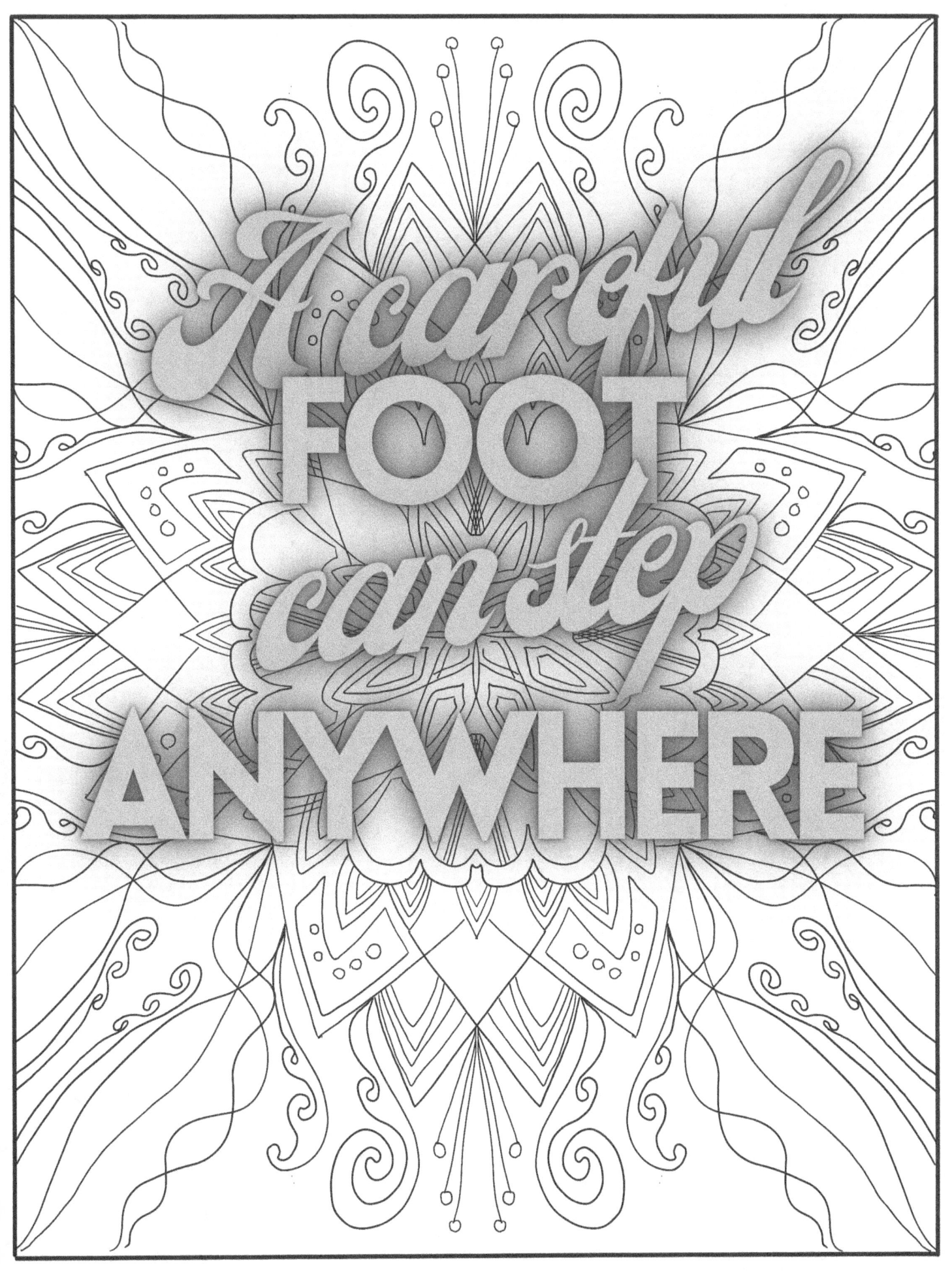

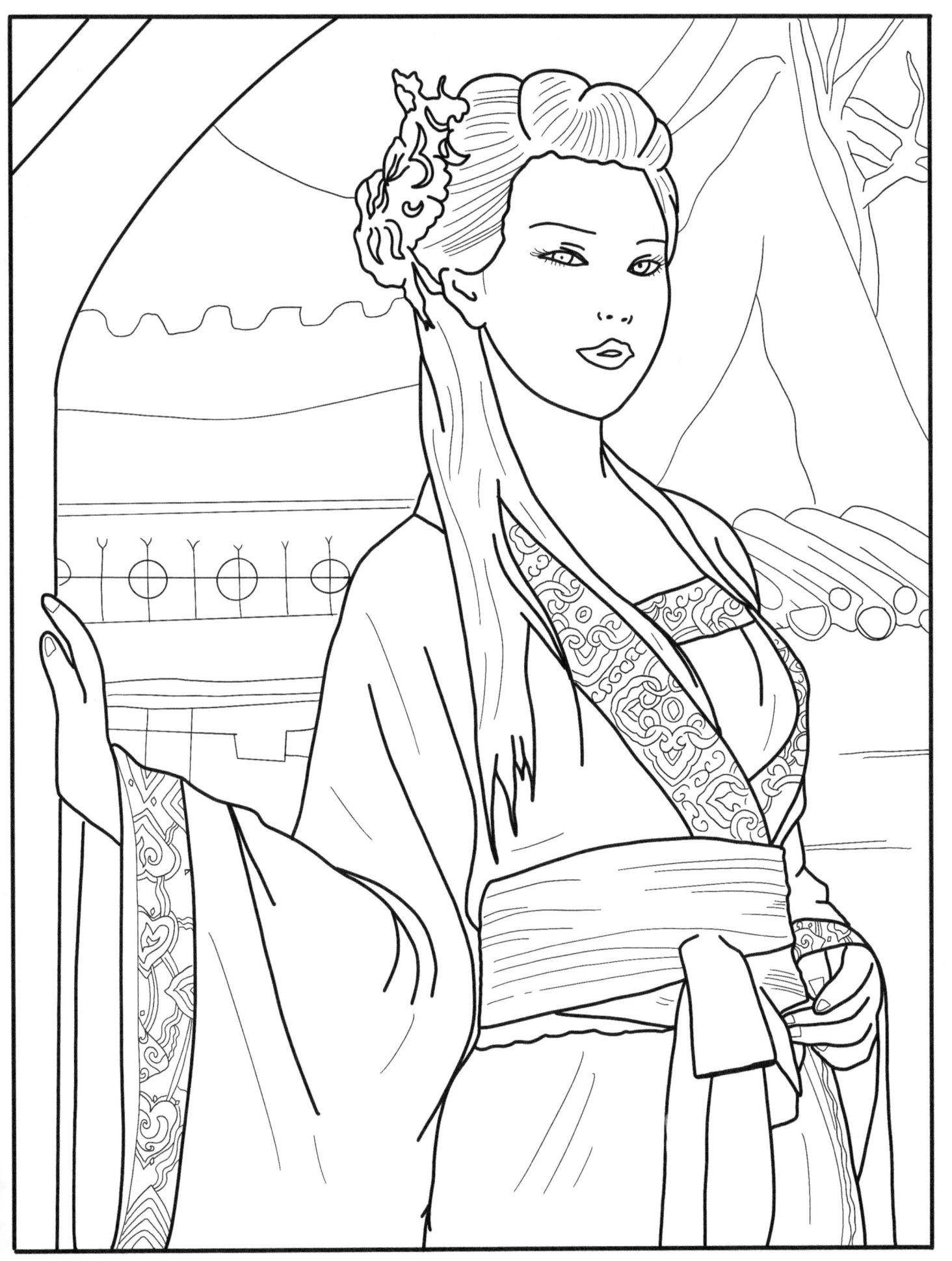

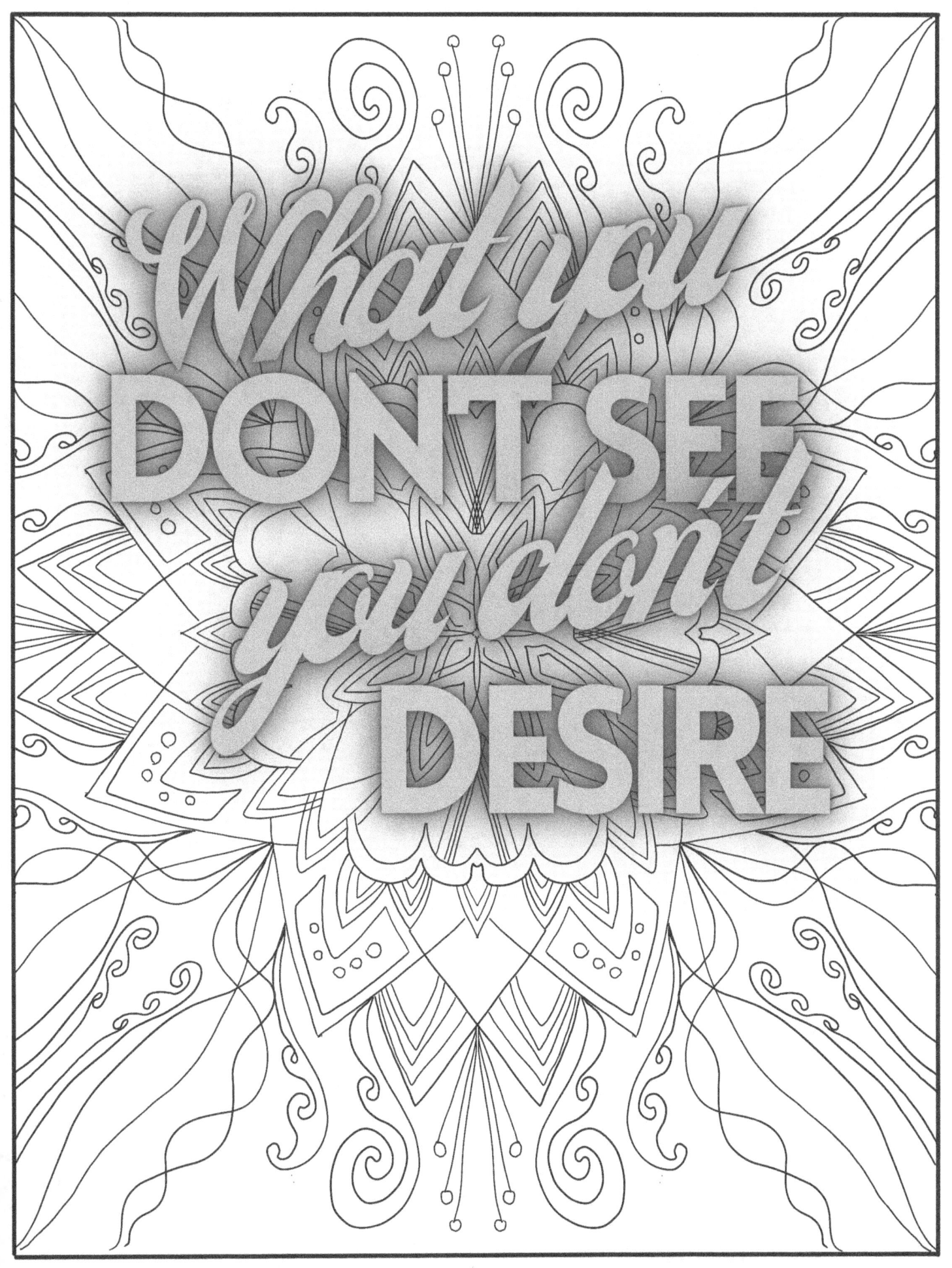

A Word of Advice:

It is wise to use a piece of paper or cardboard between
the pages to make sure you don't bleed
through to the page beneath.

This paper is **NOT MEANT** FOR **WET MEDIUMS.**

Use **Crayons** and **Colored Pencils** for
best results.

Amazon is our printer and therefore we
have **NO CONTROL** over the
paper weight used.

Thank you for your consideration.